Globalization

1977–2008

SADDLEBACK
EDUCATIONAL PUBLISHING

Saddleback's *Graphic American History*

ISBN-10: 1-59905-368-3
ISBN-13: 978-1-59905-368-4
eBook: 978-1-60291-696-8

Printed in Malaysia

20 19 18 17 16   7 8 9 10 11

On January 21, 1977, a Democrat from Georgia was sworn in as the 39th president of the United States.

His first remarks were addressed to the former president, Gerald Ford, and cheered by the crowd.

When his address ended, he surprised and delighted the crowd by walking the half-mile to the White House.

Thomas Jefferson started the tradition of the inaugural parade after his second inauguration. In 1977, Jimmy Carter was the first president to walk from the Capitol to the White House after the ceremony, symbolizing that he was a man of the people.

The Middle East was a volatile region. Israel occupied territories of other Middle Eastern countries. There was also the problem of Palestinian refugees.

As president, Carter wanted peace in the Middle East. He found that for peace to work, Israel had to withdraw from the territories that it occupied. Carter began work to create a peace plan.

During the autumn of 1978, the president invited Israel's prime minister, Menachem Begin, and Egypt's president, Anwar Sadat, to the United States to work out a peace plan.

The leaders met at Camp David, the presidential retreat outside Washington. Thirteen days of secret negotiations followed.

Finally, on September 17, 1978, the leaders of Egypt and Israel reached an agreement. The agreement came to be known as the Camp David Accords.

Late in 1979, a band of students took over the American embassy in Tehran, the capital city of Iran. Many Americans became hostages.

Although several of the hostages were released during 1980, 52 others remained in Iran.

Meanwhile, in 1980, Ronald Reagan, the former governor of California, was elected president.

As preparations for Reagan's inauguration were being made, plans for releasing the hostages were nearing completion.

Finally, on January 20, 1981, Ronald Reagan became the 40th president of the United States. At the same time, planes carrying the 52 hostages, took off from an airfield in Iran.

In his inaugural address, President Reagan spoke about the bright future of America.

We are too great a nation to limit ourselves to small dreams.

A great air of rejoicing swept the country. In Washington, D.C., great parties were held to welcome the new president.

And a few days afterward, the joy was complete when 52 smiling ex-hostages arrived home.

On March 30, 1981, as President Reagan was leaving the Washington Hilton Hotel, he was shot by John Hinckley Jr.

President Reagan was rushed to the George Washington University Hospital, where he underwent emergency surgery.

I hope you're a Republican.

Today, Mr. President, we're all Republicans.

President Reagan was not the first president to be shot. Presidents who survived assassination attempts were Andrew Jackson (1835), Theodore Roosevelt (1912), Franklin D. Roosevelt (1933), Harry S. Truman (1950), Richard M. Nixon (1972 and 1974), and Gerald R. Ford (1975).

Four United States presidents were assassinated: Abraham Lincoln (1865), James Garfield (1881), William McKinley (1901), and John F. Kennedy (1963).

6

Reagan became president during a period of high inflation and unemployment. Reagan had promised to lower taxes and reduce government spending during his election campaign.

Reagan introduced a new economic policy that came to be known as *Reaganomics*. Reagan cut government spending, reduced taxes, curbed inflation, and increased employment.

On August 3, 1981, the union representing America's air traffic controllers called a strike. President Reagan declared the strike illegal.

Let me make one thing plain. If they do not report for work within 48 hours, they will forfeit their jobs and be terminated.

Two days later, following their refusal to report for work, Reagan fired the 11,345 striking air traffic controllers.

On July 7, 1981, President Reagan nominated Sandra Day O'Connor to the United States Supreme Court.

She is truly a person for all seasons.

President Reagan had made a pledge during the election campaign that he would appoint a woman to the Supreme Court of the United States.

Sandra Day O'Connor graduated from Stanford Law School and was a former state senator and assistant attorney general of Arizona. She was a trial judge for five years and in 1979 was appointed to the Arizona Court of Appeals.

On September 25, 1981, O'Connor was sworn in as the 102nd justice of the Supreme Court. She became the first woman associate justice of the Supreme Court in American history. As a judge, she was a key figure in court decisions.

I, Sandra Day O'Connor, do solemnly swear...

The Senate confirmed O'Connor's nomination by a vote of 99-0.

On July 1, 2005, O'Connor announced her retirement. She retired on January 31, after serving for 24 years.

During the early 1980s, many homosexual men in New York and Los Angeles were getting sick with a rare type of cancer. No one knew why. In 1981, scientists identified a deadly virus called HIV or *human immunodeficiency virus.* The source of the HIV virus, however, remained a mystery.

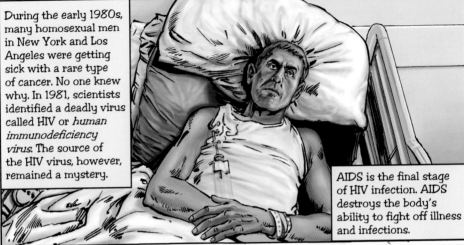

AIDS is the final stage of HIV infection. AIDS destroys the body's ability to fight off illness and infections.

During the early 1980s, as many as 150,000 people became infected with HIV each year. Scientists didn't know what people could do to protect themselves.

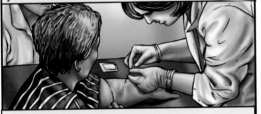

It took scientists several years to develop a blood test for the virus.

Finally, scientists were able to identify a type of chimpanzee in West Africa as the source of the HIV virus. Over several years, the virus slowly spread across Africa and into other parts of the world.

AIDS has already killed more than 500,000 American men, women, and children, and about 25 million people worldwide.

Today despite major advances in prevention and treatment for HIV/AIDS, about 40,000 people are infected with HIV each year in the United States alone. Prevention is still the only "cure" for AIDS.

The Lebanese population was mostly made up of Christians and Muslims in the 1980s. There were many disagreements between Muslims and Christians over who should rule Lebanon.

Israel and Syria also had forces in Lebanon.

In the early 1980s, armed conflict broke out between the Christian government and a number of Muslim groups. Reagan supported the Christians and sent marines to Lebanon to strengthen the Lebanese government.

On May 17, 1983, the United States, Lebanon, and Israel signed an agreement for withdrawal of Israeli troops on the condition that Syria would also withdraw its troops.

Then in October 1983, a suicide bomber killed nearly 250 marines and other Americans at their Beirut headquarters.

On March 5, 1984, the Lebanese government canceled the May 17 agreement.

Our marines departed a few weeks later.

After World War II, the United Nations recommended the partition of Palestine into two states. Arabs protested against the creation of the new state of Israel and what they considered the occupation of Palestine.

Jerusalem

Dead Sea

Gaza

Proposed Jewish State

Proposed Arab State

Internationally administered Corpus Separatum of Jerusalem

Arab nations in the Middle East wanted to reclaim the land. They formed a "liberation army" and attacked Israel.

In the years that followed, Israel occupied new lands in the West Bank and the Gaza Strip.

In 1987, Palestinians rose up in protest against the Israeli occupation. They called their uprising the Intifada.*

Ever since, there has been great hostility between Israel and its Arab neighbors.

Most countries in the world are dependent on oil from the Middle East. Therefore, a peaceful relationship with Arab nations is important for the world.

Both Arabs and Israelis have accused each other of human rights violations. This hostility has made the Middle East a volatile region.

*an Arabic word which means "to shake off."

On April 5, 1986, a bomb exploded in a disco in Berlin frequented by American service personnel.

63 American soldiers were among the 200 injured in the terror attack. One soldier and one civilian died.

President Reagan said that Libya's leader, Colonel Muammar el-Qaddafi, ordered the attack on Americans

We have irrefutable proof.

America had long been alarmed by state-sponsored terrorism. Each year, thousands of terrorists trained in Libya.

On April 16, President Reagan addressed Americans and the world. The mission, codenamed *El Dorado Canyon*, was to bomb Libya in retaliation for the Berlin attack.

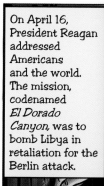

Self-defense is not only our right; it is our duty. It is the purpose behind the mission...

Sixty tons of bombs were dropped on five targets that were involved in terrorist activity.

On January 29, President Ronald Reagan announced that he would be seeking re-election.

Vice President Bush and I would like to have your continued support and cooperation in completing what we began three years ago.

In the presidential elections of 1984, President Reagan was overwhelmingly re-elected.

In this blessed land, there is always a better tomorrow.

On July 28, 1984, the city of Los Angeles hosted the Olympic Games. President Reagan officially opened the games.

I declare the 23rd Olympiad open!

Carl Lewis equaled Jesse Owens' 1936 record by winning four gold medals.

The games were a huge success, even though the Soviet Union and 14 other countries boycotted the games.

The space shuttle program was launched by Nixon in 1972. Space shuttles flew after the Apollo missions were completed in 1975.

On the morning of January 28, 1986, *Challenger* was ready to fly into space on its 10th mission.

On board was Christa McAuliffe, the first teacher to fly into space. McAuliffe's presence on *Challenger* excited the entire nation.

The other members of the crew were Francis Scobee, Michael Smith, Ronald McNair, Ellison Onizuka, Judith Resnick, and Gregory Jarvis.

Seventy-three seconds into the mission, *Challenger* seemingly exploded in midair. All crewmembers, including Christa McAuliffe were killed.

President Reagan spoke to a grieving nation.

We will never forget them, nor the last time we saw them, this morning, as they prepared for their journey and waved goodbye and slipped the surly bonds of Earth to touch the face of God.

President Reagan appointed a commission to investigate the tragic accident. The commission was headed by former secretary of state, William Roger.

The commission found that an o-ring failed, causing structural failure. The o-ring failure allowed outgassing from the solid rocket booster, which caused a massive explosion.

In November 1986, a Lebanese magazine ran a story that the United States had illegally sold arms to Iran in exchange for hostages. Iran confirmed the story. This scandal was known as *Iran-contra*.

We did not, repeat, did not trade arms or anything else for hostages.

Attorney General Meese discovered that arms were sold to Iran and the profits were used to fund contra rebels in Nicaragua.

An embarrassed Reagan appointed the Tower Commission find out what happened. Reagan testified twice to the Tower Commission but claimed to have no recollection of the events.

On February 26, 1987, the Tower Commission delivered its report to the president. The report did not find evidence that Reagan knew about the diversion of money to the contras.

On March 4, 1987, Reagan spoke to Americans on national television.

It was a mistake.

Four days before Christmas at 6:00 p.m. on December 21, 1988, Pan AM Flight 103 took off from London's Heathrow Airport headed for New York.

On board the Boeing 747 were 243 passengers and 16 crewmembers.

An hour later the plane exploded over Lockerbie, a small town in southwestern Scotland.

Eleven residents of Lockerbie were also killed by the falling debris.

Investigations revealed that Libyan terrorists blew up the plane. The terrorists planted a bomb on the plane in retaliation for the bombing of Libya.

Investigators believed that the bombers were Abdelbaset Ali Mohmed al-Megrahi and Al Amin Khalifa Fhimah, both Libyan nationals.

On January 31, 2001, 11 years after the attack, al-Megrahi was found guilty of murder and was sentenced to life in prison. Fhimah was acquitted.

After World War II the Soviets, Americans, and the British bickered over who would control which part of the former empires of Germany, Italy, and Japan.

The Soviets encouraged communism in Eastern Europe and supported Communist movements in Asia.

To counter the threat of communism, the United States created the Truman Doctrine and the Marshall Plan. Congress also passed the National Security Act, which established the Department of Defense and the CIA (Central Intelligence Agency). This was the beginning of the West's cold war with communism.

The Truman Doctrine gave economic and military support to Greece and Turkey to prevent their falling under Soviet control. The Marshall Plan was the primary plan of the United States for rebuilding and creating a stronger Western Europe and preventing a Communist takeover.

In the United States, Senator Joseph McCarthy held congressional hearings looking for Communist spies in the government.

Soviet premier Nikita Khrushchev, while addressing Western ambassadors at a reception at the Polish embassy in Moscow on November 18, 1956, remarked:

We will bury you.

During the 1950s, the threat of a nuclear war loomed large.

On November 8, 1988, Vice President George Bush won the United States presidential election. He defeated Massachusetts Governor Michael Dukakis.

On January 20, 1988, he was sworn in as the 41st president of the United States.

I, George Bush, do solemnly swear...

His first statement was addressed to Ronald Reagan.

President Reagan, on behalf of our nation, I thank you for the wonderful things that you have done for America.

After the ceremony, Bush led the inaugural parade to the White House.

He walked several blocks and greeted the crowds.

The Berlin Wall divided the city of Berlin in two halves. It was a symbol of the *iron curtain*.* It was built to stop people from crossing over to the more prosperous West.

Many people lost their lives trying to cross the wall.

On June 12, 1987, Reagan spoke from the Berlin Wall.

Mr. Gorbachev, tear down this wall!

By the end of 1990, most of the Berlin Wall was torn down.

*Term used to describe the divide between Western Europe and Soviet Bloc countries of Eastern Europe.

On March 11, 1985, Mikhail Gorbachev became the general secretary of the Communist Party of the Soviet Union.

Gorbachev represented a new generation of Soviet leaders.

Gorbachev knew that the Soviet economy was in a bad shape.

The Soviet government had alienated themselves from the people.

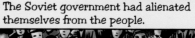

People did not have freedom. They could not speak openly about their problems.

Gorbachev was determined to change the Soviet economy and society.

We can't live like this any longer.

He also wanted to improve relations with the West, especially the United States.

His efforts would ultimately bring an end to the Cold War.

Gorbachev introduced new reforms. They were known as *glasnost* or openness and *perestroika* or reform.

Glasnost and perestroika eased tensions between the West and the Soviet Union. Reagan and the Soviets met four times from 1985 to 1988.

In November 1985, the two leaders met for the first time in Geneva. It was a historic meeting.

The leaders talked about reducing nuclear weapons. It was a positive beginning.

The next three summit meetings built the momentum for future weapons reductions. It also built trust among the leaders.

Meanwhile, Gorbachev reduced Soviet forces in Eastern Europe.

In 1989, he ordered the withdrawal of Soviet forces from Afghanistan.

The same year, countries in Eastern Europe saw the collapse of Communist regimes and the Soviet Empire.

Finally, on July 31, 1991, Gorbachev and President Bush signed a treaty to reduce nuclear weapons by a third.

On Christmas 1991, the Soviet Union finally dissolved to form the Commonwealth of Independent States or CIS. The cold war was officially over.

On the night of March 24, 1989, the *Exxon Valdez*, an oil tanker, hit a reef off the Alaskan coast and ran aground. The tanker leaked oil into the ocean.

Over the next two days, the *Exxon Valdez* would spill 38 million liters (84 million gallons) of oil into the ocean.

The clean-up operation was slow because Exxon was unprepared for such an accident.

The oil slick would eventually coat more than 1,100 miles of the Alaskan coastline making it one of the largest spills in United States history.

The *Exxon Valdez* spill was one of the largest ecological disasters. The oil slick killed thousands of nesting shorebirds and sea mammals.

As of 2008, the natural population still has not recovered from the disaster.

Carbon dioxide (CO_2) is a greenhouse gas. It is one of the main causes of environmental pollution. Only 5% of the world's population lives in the United States, but the United States contributes 22% of the world's carbon emissions.*

The burning of fossil fuels is the single biggest contributor to environmental pollution. The United States is the largest consumer of fossil fuels, using about 25% of the world's resources.

Personal cars and trucks emit 20% of the United States' carbon emissions.

More than 85% of the world's energy consumption is through the burning of fossil fuels.

Air pollutants that come from the burning of fossil fuels for electricity production, industrial use, home heating, and transportation also cause disease and ailments in humans.

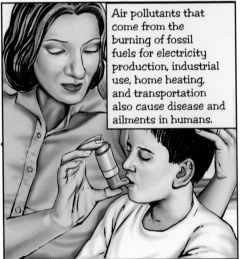

*Emissions are gases and particles released into the air

Shortly after midnight on August 2, 1990, Iraq suddenly and without warning attacked Kuwait.

By dawn, the Iraqi army occupied the capital and most of the country. Iraq claimed Kuwait as its 19th province.

Saudi Arabia feared that it would be invaded next and asked for American help.

President Bush asked Iraqi President, Saddam Hussein, to withdraw unconditionally. He also sent American troops into Saudi Arabia, and the United States Navy moved into the Persian Gulf.

Four days later, the United Nations imposed economic sanctions on Iraq. At the same time a large contingent of coalition forces were assembling in Saudi Arabia.

On November 29, the United Nations gave a January 15, 1991, deadline to Iraq to withdraw or face military action.

As the deadline neared, military forces from 32 nations assembled in Saudi Arabia. The force included 650,000 troops.

The Iraqis refused to withdraw from Kuwait.

Kuwait is a part of Iraq.

On January 17, American-led coalition forces began air raids on Iraq. The air raids would continue for the next 43 days.

On February 24, 1991, ground forces began moving into Kuwait and Iraq. The coalition forces destroyed the Iraqi army.

Two days later, Iraq announced the withdrawal of its troops from Kuwait. By then 100,000 Iraqis were dead and 150,000 wounded. Unfortunately, fleeing Iraqi soldiers set fire to oil fields.

On February 28, 1991, President Bush declared victory.

Kuwait is liberated. This is a victory for all humankind.

In the 1992 presidential election, Bush faced a young Democratic challenger from Arkansas, Bill Clinton. Bill Clinton chose Tennessee Senator Al Gore as his running mate.

Do you trust the Democrats to stand up to the Russians?

On November 3, Bill Clinton was elected as the 42nd president. He received 43% of the popular vote, while Bush received 37%.

Bill Clinton was sworn in as president on January 21, 1993.

I, William Jefferson Clinton, do solemnly swear...

Later, he addressed the nation.

To renew America, we must meet challenges abroad, as well as at home.

On February 26, 1993, Eyad Ismoil drove a yellow Ford van into the basement of the World Trade Center North Tower. Ramzi Yousef was also with him in the truck.

The Ford van was no ordinary truck. In all, 680 kilograms (1,500 pounds) of explosives were loaded inside.

The two men set the bomb timer to 12:18 p.m. and walked out of the basement.

The bomb exploded. The explosion was so powerful that it created a crater several stories deep in the North Tower.

There's so much smoke!

Over the next few hours, people were evacuated from the Twin Towers. Many people were trapped as smoke rose through the buildings.

Six people died and more than a thousand were injured in the attack.

I can't breathe.

On February 28, 1993, agents from the Bureau of Alcohol, Tobacco, and Firearms (ATF) raided the compound of a small religious community called the Branch Davidians near Waco, Texas. A gunfight broke out. Four ATF agent died plus an unknown number of Branch Davidians.

The Branch Davidians were accused of illegally possessing arms and explosives.

David Koresh, the leader of the Branch Davidians, was also accused of child abuse.

Following the raid, the FBI took charge and blockaded the compound.

The blockade continued for 51 days.

On April 19, the FBI launched a full military-style assault on the Branch Davidians. Armored vehicles tore holes in the main building and tear gas was used.

As the tanks were driving around the compound, a fire broke out.

The fire raged for 40 minutes and burned everything to the ground. About 80 Branch Davidians were killed in the assault, including 22 children.

Exactly two years after the Waco siege, a powerful car bomb exploded at the Alfred Murrah Federal Building in Oklahoma City.

The bomb destroyed most of the 9-story building. In all, 168 people, including 19 children were killed in the explosion.

Within days, it became clear that the bomb was planted by Timothy McVeigh, a former soldier.

McVeigh held the ATF and FBI responsible for the Waco massacre.

The Murrah building held many federal offices, including the offices of the ATF and FBI.

Timothy McVeigh was found guilty and executed by lethal injection on June 11, 2001.

Clinton's presidency saw the revival of the American economy. The longest period of economic growth in United States history occurred during the Clinton administration.

But his presidency was plagued with scandals and charges of ethical lapses. The first major scandal was in the fall of 1993.

What about this Whitewater thing?

It's about a real estate deal and partnership gone wrong.

During his investigation, independent counsel Kenneth Starr learned that Clinton had an inappropriate relationship with a young female intern at the White House.

Who is this intern?

Her name is Monica Lewinsky.

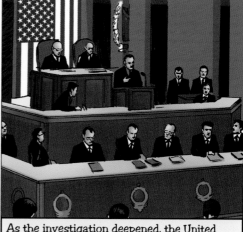

As the investigation deepened, the United States House of Representatives impeached President Clinton.

The Clinton administration enacted many new reforms. One such reform was the Family and Medical Leave Act. The law allowed an employee to take unpaid leave for the following reasons: due to the birth of a child; to take care of an immediate family member who had a serious health condition; in case of a serious personal health condition where the employee was unable to perform his or her job.

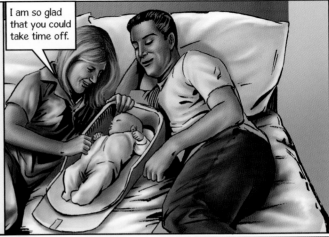

I am so glad that you could take time off.

Now Americans must wait up to five days for a background check before being allowed to purchase a handgun.

Gun violence was increasingly being seen as a social evil that America could do without. The Clinton administration sought to control this menace. On November 30, 1993, President Clinton signed into law the Brady Bill.

The Clinton administration negotiated NAFTA. It was an agreement for free trade between the United States, Canada, and Mexico. NAFTA became effective in 1994.

The Clinton administration also worked for the creation of new jobs so that there were fewer unemployed Americans. Many welfare reforms were started, and for the first time in 30 years, Clinton submitted a balanced U.S. budget.

In 1969, a pioneering computer science professor at UCLA, Leonard Kleinrock, and a small group of his students logged onto a Stanford University computer.

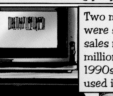

Yes, we see the L.

Do you see the L?

A revolution in human communication had begun. This was the birth of the Internet. This early Internet was called ARPANET. In the early days of the Internet, there were no personal computers. Computer experts, engineers, scientists, and librarians were the only people who used the ARPANET.

In 1981, another revolution took place with the invention of the IBM personal computer. At the same time, Microsoft developed DOS, an operating system for the IBM personal computer. DOS made it easier for people to use computers.

Two million personal computers were sold in 1981. The next year sales more than doubled to 5.5 million. By the beginning of the 1990s, 65 million PCs were being used in homes, offices, and schools.

In 1990, the ARPANET ceased to exist. Now anyone with a personal computer and Internet connection could log onto the Internet.

New technology companies made huge profits from the growth of the Internet and the rising sale of personal computers.

The value of technology stocks grew rapidly. The stock market was unstoppable. By 1999, the Dow Jones had doubled in value.

This is the time to invest in technology stocks.

In the 1990s, the Internet grew by 100% every year. Millions of users were using the Internet everyday. 1996 was a remarkable year for technology. The Internet saw an explosive growth in users around the world.

It's easy to do research for my term paper online.

Internet services and media companies like America Online and Yahoo! were on their way to becoming Internet giants.

In 1996, Yahoo! was serving more than 100 million users worldwide.

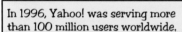

WELCOME TO THE
YAHOO!
STOCKHOLDERS' MEETING

By November 1996, America Online users were sending 5 million emails a day.

The world is becoming a global village.

In 1996, new technologies helped users to share and find information easily. New technologies, such as inter-linked hypertext documents, email, online chat, file transfer and file sharing, and online gaming helped people to interact, learn, and communicate easily.

Hotmail was launched in 1996. Google was launched in 1998.

This is the *New York Times* website.

Many traditional businesses also joined in the technological revolution. In 1996, the Internet created 1.1 million new jobs worldwide.

New advances in technology made e-commerce services available on the Internet. These new services allowed users to find, connect, sell, or buy on the Internet.

It's so easy to Christmas shop at home!

The Internet and technology is changing our lives everyday. We search online for the best price. We buy cars online. We read newspapers online. We blog. We rarely use "snail mail." We send emails.

New technologies also made transactions safe and secure over the Internet.

One such technology is SSL or Secure Socket Layer. SSL is an encryption technology that scrambles important data such as credit card numbers when it is being stored or passed from one computer to another.

Technologies like online auctions made the Internet a marketplace where users can bid and bargain.

I'm going to bid $23.50.

Internet companies like eBay are at the forefront of this technology.

Apple's personal digital media players, iPods, have revolutionized the way people entertain themselves.

I'm comin' up so you better get this party started...

On the morning of August 7, 1998, the American embassies in Nairobi and Dar es Salaam came under attack simultaneously. Cars packed with explosives detonated outside the embassies.

In Nairobi, 212 people are killed and about 4,000 were injured in the car-bomb explosion.

In Dar es Salaam, 11 people were killed and 85 were injured in the attack. The attacks were carried out by Osama Bin Laden's terrorist organization *Al Qaeda*.

In 2000, as the USS *Cole* was refueling, two suicide bombers rammed a small boat packed with explosives into the destroyer. Seventeen sailors died and 39 were injured in the attack.

The Republican nominee for the 2000 presidential election was George W. Bush.

I want to help people who help themselves.

The Democratic Party nominated Vice President Al Gore.

You ain't seen nothing yet.

On November 7, 2000, Americans went to the polls to elect their new president. Al Gore won the popular vote by 543,816 votes.

Tallahassee

Orlando

Miami

But there was a dispute over Florida's 25 electoral votes.

Finally, Bush was declared the winner in Florida. He became the 43rd president of the country.

On January 21, 2001, George W. Bush was sworn in as president.

I will faithfully execute the office of the president of the United States.

He was the first president since 1888 who failed to win the popular vote.

He addressed the nation.

A single nation of justice and opportunity...

Thousands of people took part in the inaugural parade.

That's the Texas Longhorn Band.

A block from the White House, the president and his wife got out of the limousine and walked the last hundred feet.

On the morning of September 11, 2001, four Boeing passenger jets were hijacked by 19 Arab terrorists armed with knives, box-cutters, mace, and pepper spray.

At 8:46 a.m., an airplane with 92 people on board crashed into the World Trade Center's North Tower. The impact was so great that 600 people were instantly killed. The airplane was American Airlines Flight 11, hijacked while flying from Boston to Los Angeles.

At 9:03 a.m., another plane crashed into the South Tower of the World Trade Center. This second airplane was United Airlines Flight 175 with 65 people on board.

At 9:37 a.m., American Airlines Flight 77 crashed into the Pentagon, killing 125 military officers and civilians and all 64 people including five hijackers aboard the flight.

Around the same time, the Federal Aviation Administration grounded all flights in the United States.

This was the first time in United States history that air traffic nationwide was halted. People were stranded across the country.

At 9:59 a.m., the South Tower of the World Trade Center collapsed.

The North Tower followed at 10:28 a.m. Hundreds of firefighters and police died during the rescue attempt.

At 9:58 a.m., emergency operators in Pennsylvania received a call from a passenger on board United Airlines Flight 93.

We're being hijacked! We're being hijacked!

One minute after the call began, the line died.

At about 10:03 a.m., United 93 crashed into an open field in Shanksville, Pennsylvania.

United Airlines Flight 93 was flying from Newark to San Francisco with 44 people on board.

News of the attack created fear. All important buildings and skyscrapers throughout the country were evacuated.

America is under attack!

We need to evacuate lower Manhattan.

Al Qaeda, a terrorist group based in Afghanistan, was responsible for the 9/11 attack. Al Qaeda's leader, bin Laden, became the most wanted terrorist in the world.

Later, President Bush spoke to the nation.

Make no mistake, the United States will hunt down and punish those responsible for these cowardly acts.

On October 26, 2001, following the tragic events of September 11, President Bush signed into law an act that gave enforcement agencies more power to fight terrorism in the United States.

We have to act. We can't hope for the best anymore.

What's in this Patriot Act?

Now the government can search our telephone and email records without a court order.

That's not good.

On March 1, 2003, the Bush administration created the Department of Homeland Security (DHS) to deal with the threat of terrorism.

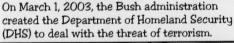

This department is going to make our country safe for everyone.

Twenty-two federal agencies, including the former INS, Coast Guard, and Federal Emergency Management Agency were merged to create the Department of Homeland Security.

Two days before the 9/11 attacks, General Ahmed Massoud, the leader of the Northern Alliance, was killed in a daring attack by Al Qaeda suicide bombers in Afghanistan.

Since 1996, Afghanistan was under the rule of the Taliban. Bin Laden's special forces were providing support to the Taliban militia to fight the Afghan civil war with the Northern Alliance.

After the 9/11 attacks, the United States asked the Taliban to arrest bin Laden and hand him over to the United States.

The United States then formed an international anti-terrorism coalition. Massoud's Northern Alliance also became a partner in this new war on terror.

The Taliban refused.

On October 7, American and British forces launched air attacks against the Taliban and Al Qaeda in Afghanistan.

Helped by the bombings, the Northern Alliance soon captured the capital city of Kabul and other important cities. By January 2002, the Taliban and Al Qaeda were largely defeated.

Terrorism and violence are against the teaching of Islam, a religion that stands for peace, respect for human dignity, dialogue, and tolerance.

In early December, a United Nations sponsored conference appointed Hamid Karzai as Afghanistan's interim leader.

After the Gulf War, the UN-imposed economic embargo caused extreme hardship and poverty in Iraq. In 1995, the UN allowed Iraq to export limited quantities of oil to pay for food and medicines.

But Iraq diverted part of the income from this program to weapons development.

Iraq was linked to an attempted assassination of former United States President George H. W. Bush. Iraq was also thought to support known terrorist groups.

Following the 9/11 attacks, President Bush made clear that he wanted to remove Saddam Hussein.

By the end of 2002, the United States was planning an invasion of Iraq. National Security Adviser Condoleezza Rice briefed the press.

There clearly are contacts between Al Qaeda and Iraq.

Iraq continues to shelter and support terrorist organizations.

Simply stated, there is no doubt that Saddam Hussein now has weapons of mass destruction.

The United States believed that Iraq possessed chemical and biological weapons. It also believed that Hussein was actively pursuing a nuclear weapons program.

In October 2002, the United States obtained a United Nations resolution authorizing inspections of Iraqi weapons facilities.

The inspectors found no evidence that Iraq possessed any nuclear capability.

On March 17, 2003, President Bush asked Saddam Hussein to leave Iraq within 48 hours.

The day of your liberation is near.

On the evening of March 18, American and British forces began their attack. Their target was a building in Baghdad where Saddam Hussein and other top officials were meeting.

Saddam Hussein escaped unhurt.

Iraqi forces were first attacked with cruise missiles. Then the allies bombed Baghdad.

American and British troops advanced from Kuwait northward, taking the port city of Umm Qasr and the Fao Peninsula and besieging Basra.

By April 9, the United States was in control of Baghdad.

Hurrah!

Hurrah!

A small but enthusiastic crowd cheered as marines helped them tear down a statue of Saddam in the city center.

On May 1, 2003, President Bush declared the war over.

In the battle of Iraq, the United States and our allies have prevailed.

On February 1, 2003, tragedy struck NASA's first space shuttle *Columbia*.

Columbia was on its 28th mission in space. The shuttle disintegrated during re-entry over Texas, killing all seven astronauts.

The first sign of danger came at 8:53 a.m., when ground controllers lost data from four temperature indicators on the left side of the space shuttle. Because the shuttle was functioning normally, the crew was not alerted.

During the next four minutes, all data from the sensors was lost. Communication was lost just as mission control alerted the crew.

Columbia, Houston. We see your tire-pressure messages. We did not copy your last.

Roger... erm...

NASA officials tried desperately to reestablish communication with *Columbia*.

At that time, *Columbia* was about 207,000 feet over north-central Texas and traveling at 18 times the speed of sound.

When the shuttle did not appear as scheduled, NASA declared an emergency. The president was informed.

Around 9:00 a.m., Texas and Louisiana residents reported a loud noise and bright balls in the sky.

Columbia is lost, there are no survivors.

In 2014, the Orion project, a new generation of spacecraft, will carry astronauts into space.

Since the early 1980s, Americans have witnessed some major advances in medical technology.

Examples of advances in medical technology include new medical and surgical procedures like angioplasty and joint replacements and the invention of new drugs and medical devices.

New advances in prescription drugs have helped to reduce drug-induced side effects.

PRESCRIPTIONS

Medical breakthroughs in imaging like CT scanners became widely available during the 1980s.

Advances in CT scanner technology have led to early and more accurate diagnosis of diseases and medical conditions. This has ensured minimal invasive surgeries and improved patient recovery times.

The only treatment for cancer until recently was chemotherapy, which kills all growing cells, both good and bad. Now doctors are slowly replacing chemotherapy with "targeted" cancer drugs designed to block the deadly effects of specific genetic mutations.

New gene therapy drugs like *Herceptin*, which treats certain breast tumors, and *Gleevec* for rare leukemia, led the way.

Global warming is the increase in the average temperature of the Earth's surface. Over the past 100 years, the Earth has warmed by about 1° F.

A warmer Earth means frequent heat waves, rising sea levels, floods, droughts, wildfires, and epidemics.

According to the World Health Organization (WHO), 5 million fall ill and 150,000 people die every year because of climate-related changes.

The last 25 years were the warmest in the United States.

Scientists have shown that the increased emissions of greenhouse gases and other chemicals such as methane, nitrous oxide, and halocarbons are making the Earth hotter.

On February 16, 2005, the Kyoto Protocol came into effect. The protocol is a set of new rules and laws that will help to reduce greenhouse gas emissions across the globe.

Former Vice President Al Gore presented a documentary film about global warming at the 2006 Sundance Film Festival.

I don't really consider this a political issue. I consider it to be a moral issue.

Gore also released a book on the occasion *An Inconvenient Truth: The Planetary Emergency of Global Warming and What We Can Do About It.* The book became the number one bestseller on the *New York Times* bestseller list in 2006.

I've been trying to tell this story for a long time, and I feel as if I've failed to get the message across.

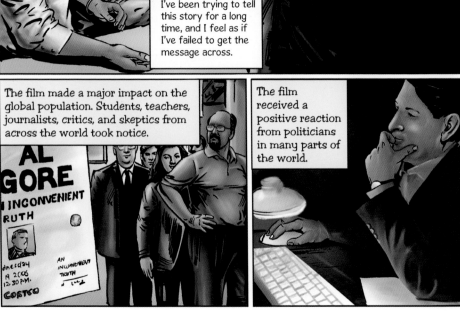

The film made a major impact on the global population. Students, teachers, journalists, critics, and skeptics from across the world took notice.

The film received a positive reaction from politicians in many parts of the world.

In the 2004 presidential election, President George W. Bush faced Democratic challenger John Kerry.

We are standing to staying on the offensive, striking terrorists abroad so we do not have to face them here at home.

As president, I will restore trust and credibility to the White House.

On Tuesday, November 2, 2004, America went to the polls in the 55th consecutive election for the president and vice president of the United States

President Bush won the election with 50.7% of the popular vote and carried 31 states.

I'm humbled by the trust and the confidence.

Bush's popularity as a "wartime" president helped him win. However, the election campaign also highlighted the negative partisan politics that had crept into mainstream America.

On January 20, 2005, President Bush was sworn in for the second time.

President Bush declared.

From all of you, I have asked patience in the hard task of securing America, which you have granted in good measure.

A massive and powerful hurricane swept through parts of Florida, Louisiana, and Mississippi in August 2005. The storm was given the name *Katrina.*

Katrina formed on August 23 during the 2005 Atlantic hurricane season. It was the fourth major storm of 2005.

When Katrina crossed southern Florida on August 25, it was a moderate hurricane, causing nine deaths and flooding.

Katrina strengthened rapidly in the Gulf of Mexico to become one of the strongest hurricanes on record.

The National Hurricane Center warned that Katrina could reach dangerous category 4 intensity before making landfall in Mississippi or Louisiana.

On August 28, Katrina became a category 5 hurricane, the worst and highest category.

President Bush declared a state of emergency in Mississippi.

The federal government in Washington, D.C., failed to recognize the scope of the problem and was slow to respond to the unfolding tragedy.

On August 29, Katrina made landfall as a category 3 hurricane in southern Plaquemines Parish.

In New Orleans, two major flood-control levees were breached. Entire neighborhoods were flooded and many people were feared dead.

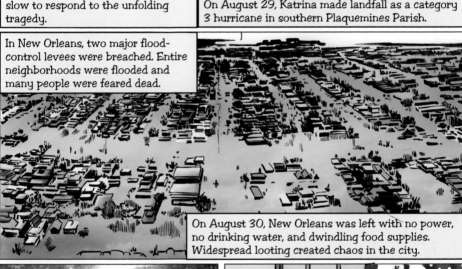

On August 30, New Orleans was left with no power, no drinking water, and dwindling food supplies. Widespread looting created chaos in the city.

On August 31, thousands of National Guard troops were deployed to New Orleans to help in rescue operations and restore order. The Bush administration was deeply criticized for failing to act quickly.

Congress approved $10.5 billion in aid for rescue and relief operations. President George W. Bush signed the bill.

The presidential primaries to choose the Republican and Democratic nominees for president began after the November 7, 2006, midterm elections.

In the following four months, eight candidates declared their intentions to run as Democrats. They were Barack Obama, Hillary Clinton, John Edwards, Joe Biden, Chris Dodd, Mike Gravel, Bill Richardson, and Dennis Kucinich.

I have fought against excessive spending and outrages. I have fought to reduce the earmarks and eliminate them.

We have had over the last eight years the biggest increases in deficit spending and national debt in our history.

Hillary Rodham Clinton and Barack Hussein Obama soon became the front runners. It was a historic primary with victory going to Obama. The Republican Party nomination went to Senator John McCain.

Barack Obama was elected as 44th president of the United States. Obama received 52% of the popular vote and 364 electoral votes as of November 7, 2008.